Cape Cod
PERSPECTIVES

Text & Photography by Douglas Congdon-Martin

Schiffer Publishing Ltd®

4880 Lower Valley Road, Atglen, Pennsylvania 19310

Title page: This topiary sign welcomes visitors as they cross the Bourne Bridge.

Right: Oyster Pond, Chatham.

Published by Schiffer Publishing Ltd.
4880 Lower Valley Road
Atglen, PA 19310
Phone: (610) 593-1777; Fax: (610) 593-2002
E-mail: Info@schifferbooks.com

For the largest selection of fine reference books on this and related subjects,
please visit our web site at **www.schifferbooks.com**
We are always looking for people to write books on new and related subjects.
If you have an idea for a book please contact us at the above address.

This book may be purchased from the publisher.
Include $3.95 for shipping.
Please try your bookstore first.
You may write for a free catalog.

In Europe, Schiffer books are distributed by
Bushwood Books
6 Marksbury Ave.
Kew Gardens
Surrey TW9 4JF England
Phone: 44 (0) 20 8392-8585; Fax: 44 (0) 20 8392-9876
E-mail: info@bushwoodbooks.co.uk
Website: www.bushwoodbooks.co.uk
Free postage in the U.K., Europe; air mail at cost.

Designed by Douglas Congdon-Martin
Type set in Humanst521 Lt BT/Zurich BT
ISBN: 978-0-7643-2766-7
Printed in China
Designed in the U.S.A.

Introduction

It's been nearly 35 years since I first stepped foot on Cape Cod. A lot has changed since then...and a lot hasn't. There are more cars on the road and a lot more cursing going on. New neighborhoods have been carved out of once open fields or verdant woods. New highways have been built to carry ever-growing numbers of people on and off the Cape, and every year a new crop of retail stores springs up to serve the needs and desires of tourists and natives alike.

It is not only people who have changed the Cape. Nature herself has had a hand in it. Every wave subtly shapes to the shoreline, depositing sand here, taking it away over there. Occasionally, when a tempest arises from the North-east or a hurricane pounds against the shoreline, major shifts in real estate can take place overnight. Dunes are erased, taking with them everything that stood upon their sweeping cliffs. Even lighthouses are consumed by the sea, if they are not moved through the Herculean efforts of those who love them.

And yet, as much as things have changed during my experience of Cape Cod, some things about it remain unchanged. Despite the impositions of humanity and nature, it is still possible to find a quiet spot by the shore and watch the sun sparkle on the water. On foggy nights the mist is still penetrated by the mournful foghorns and the light, diffused and softened, plays on once familiar scenes making them phantasmagoric.

The Cape Cod of the past is never more than a turn away. By leaving the thoroughfares and highways, and venturing onto the tree-lined lanes that crisscross the Cape, you find yourself surrounded by homes and farms that have withstood all that the environment could throw at them. Usually lovingly kept, often by families who have lived in them for many generations, they are living recollections of the beautiful simplicity of Cape Cod architecture, and testaments to the skill of their creators and the grit of those who followed.

Occasionally these lanes come to a crossroad, and there, as likely as not, you will find a village. At its center may be a general store, a post office and town hall, and almost certainly a white church...the almost stereotypical, but oh so real Cape Cod town. Of course, today the store might serve Dunkin' Donuts or Starbucks coffee, but its purpose is largely unchanged from 100 years ago. It is a place where people meet to talk about the weather, catch up on gossip, and complain about all the summer folk!

Before I get too bogged down in nostalgia, let me also add that the Cape has plenty to offer our modern sensibilities. For those on the go, there is great food, theater, night life, music, shopping, antiques, art, and bookstores. Hyannis, the largest town on the Cape, is home to many of the stores and outlets you may have at home. But if you are looking for something different (you are on vacation after all!) the smaller towns offer a myriad of boutiques and shopping experiences you will find no where else.

For those whose interests lie in nature and sports, opportunities abound. Nature trails, the Massachusetts Audubon Society and other wildlife sanctuaries, bike paths, horseback riding, kayak and boat rentals, scuba diving...the list is nearly endless. And if you are more of a fan than a player, the Cape Cod League baseball program has attracted the best college players from around the country to play baseball in Cape towns. The games are free and you can find one somewhere almost every night in June, July, and early August.

The purpose of this book is to capture some of Cape Cod for you. It roughly follows a course from the Bourne Bridge at Buzzard's Bay, out to Provincetown on the Bay side via Route 6A, and back through Chatham, Hyannis, and Falmouth via Route 28. The limitations of paper and ink mean that I am not able to convey the sound of the waves crashing against the shore or the seagull's cry. Nor will you be able to feel the wind blow across the water and into your face or smell its saltiness. Most sadly, at least for me, you will not be able to taste fresh boiled lobster or steamed clams, or feel the dribble of melted butter down your chin.

I hope, though, that these Cape Cod perspectives will trigger a memory or unearth a feeling, recalling your days on this wonderful peninsula.

—Douglas Congdon-Martin

Previous page: Near the mouth of the Cape Cod Canal at the Massachusetts Maritime Academy, facing the Cape Cod Canal Railroad Bridge. The canal bridges were built between 1933 and 1935.

Above: The Bourne Bridge, at the west end of the Cape Cod Canal, and its twin sister Sagamore Bridge at the east end, carry thousands of visitors to the Cape each year.

Right: The roads along either side of the Canal are quite scenic, but the best view is on the walking/bicycle paths that run beside the canal just a few feet above the water level.

The Dexter Grist Mill is a working mill that has served Sandwich on Shawme Pond since 1654. The 54 inch French Burl millstone still grinds corn, which is available to tourists.

Several historic homes surround Shawme Pond, including the Thornton Burgess house and museum, the Hoxie House shown on the next page, and this beauty, the Newcomb Tavern, just across the water from the mill. Built in 1693, it served as the center for the local Tories in revolutionary days, while the Fessenden Tavern, on the site of today's Daniel Webster Inn, was the meeting place for the Patriots.

As one would expect at the Cape's oldest town, history abounds in Sandwich. Around the pond from the Grist Mill stands the Hoxie House, among the oldest on Cape Cod. It was built in 1637 and was still occupied, but without electricity, in the 1950s when the town purchased it.

For those who wish to own a bit of history, Sandwich offers several shops. The Sandwich Auction House, in business since 1974, has auctions almost weekly, year-round. In the summer they are on Wednesday evenings.

The bookseller at Titcomb's Book Shop in East Sandwich has been welcoming bibliophiles to their wonderful collection of new and rare books for over 35 years.

Route 6A is bounded on each side by tidal marshes. Ecologically, they support a wide variety of plant and animal life. Recreationally, they are great places for nature walks, swimming, and kayaking. In every way they are places of great beauty.

The Giving Tree Gallery on Route 6A in East Sandwich was opened in the late 1980s. It has four acres of sculpture gardens and nature paths, including a great hanging bridge that carries one into the tidal marshes. In addition to the wonderful sculpture they handle outdoors, the shop features art jewelry of the highest caliber.

As Route 6A goes into West Barnstable, you will pass the beautiful barn and gardens of Claire Murray Hand Hooked Rugs. The barn has been honored by the Historical Society of Cape Cod for its preservation and restoration, and the gardens are a prime example of wonderful horticulture that abounds on the Cape. The shop includes finished rugs, kits, and supplies, and courses in rug hooking are offered throughout the year.

West Barnstable offers a wonderful array of activities, from a relaxed mid-morning coffee break at an outdoor café to oil painting instruction at the Cape Cod Art Association.

It is also the home of the Barnstable County Court House, designed by Alexander Parris and built in 1832. The statue is of Mercy Otis Warren, a writer and poet, and among the important women of the American Revolution. She was a native of West Barnstable.

The Barnstable Harbor is home to fishing boats and pleasure craft alike. In season, whale watch cruises leave from the harbor.

In the distance is Sandy Neck Light, which began its sentry of Barnstable Harbor in 1857, replacing an earlier wooden structure with a 34 foot tower of brick. The light was decommissioned and the lantern removed in 1931.

Left: Lothrop Hill Cemetery in West Barnstable dates back to 1653 when Rev. John Lothrop was buried there. Historic cemeteries abound on the Cape and, in addition to pleasant rolling hills and ancient trees, they give visitors a sense of the long history of the area.

At the other end of town is the Cobb Hill Cemetery, whose rolling hills contain graves dating back to 1715.

Left: The original church built on this Cobb's Hill site in the early eighteenth century was the East Parish church. Becoming Unitarian in the early 1800s, the building was replaced in 1836 and served until 1905 when it was destroyed by fire. The current building was designed by Guy Lowell, architect of the Museum of Fine Arts in Boston, and continues to serve the community.

Top: The Cape Cod Art Association was founded in 1948 to serve artists and the community. It has three galleries and is a great place to find work by Cape Cod artists. It also offers classes in a variety of the fine arts year-round, open to members and visitors.

Above: The Coast Guard Heritage Museum is housed in the old U.S. Customshouse, now known as the Trayser Museum. Designed by Ammi Burnham Young, Supervising Architect of the Treasury, it is in the Renaissance Revival style and was built in 1856.

Opposite: A Yarmouthport gazebo.

Yarmouthport is a quiet village of extraordinary and diverse homes and shops. It is anchored at one end by Hallet's, an old-fashioned soda fountain housed in an antique apothecary shop. At the other end is Parnassus Book Service, the stereotypical old bookstore with its shelves reaching to the ceiling with literary gems, new and rare. In between there are several interesting boutiques and antiques shops. Route 6A is the town's Main Street and it is lined with a number of interesting and beautiful homes in a variety of styles, ranging from traditional Capes and garrisons to gingerbread and Greek Revival.

Scargo Tower stands atop Scargo Hill in East Dennis. It was built in 1902 and given to the town of Dennis in 1929. The hill has an elevation of 160 feet and the tower stands 28 feet above that, providing a grand view of the Cape Cod Bay. On a clear day, Provincetown can be seen in the distance.

Below the tower lies Scargo Lake, one of many bodies of fresh water around the Cape. In the summer it is a popular recreation spot.

On a beautiful campus at the center of Dennis are the Cape Cod Art Museum and The Dennis Playhouse. Founded in 1981, the Museum offers a view of the history of art on Cape Cod and showcases the work of contemporary artists. Displayed inside are both the permanent collection and special exhibits. Outside is a sculpture garden featuring works by many notable artists. These include "Aurora," a work in steel by kinetic sculptor Jerome Kirk, 1980. It was a gift to the museum by Mr. & Mrs. Irving W. Rabb.

Across the way is the Cape Playhouse, "America's Oldest Professional Summer Theater," founded in 1927. Among its performers have been Tallulah Bankhead, Humphrey Bogart, Bette Davis, Paulette Goddard, Julie Harris, Helen Hayes, Gertrude Lawrence, Gregory Peck, Ginger Rogers, and Lana Turner. In a typical season, six plays are offered, covering a variety of theatrical forms.

Also on the campus is the Cape Cinema, a single screen theater featuring a massive, 6400 square foot ceiling mural by Rockwell Kent. Founded in 1930, since 1978 the Cape Cinema has been an "Art House," specializing in independent American and international films.

The smock-style, Higgins Farm windmill stands sentry at Drummer Boy Park in Brewster on Route 6A. It was built in the 1790s at Ellis Landing and moved here in 1974. In full, working condition, it has its original millstone and many of the original timbers.

The First Parish Brewster, Unitarian-Universalist Church stands at the center of town.

Built in 1852 as a church and converted to a general store in 1866, the Brewster Store has served the community through five owners. It still offers groceries and other general merchandise, but the fine collection of penny candy is what draws the children. Their parents are likely to find a nice memento of their visit to the Cape or a good cup of coffee.

The beach at Brewster has a long, shallow tidal run, making it a favorite of families with children. Its location on the Bay means the water is usually quiet and warm.

The Cape Cod Museum of Natural History in Brewster is situated on 80 acres and abuts 300 acres of natural preserve. It has developed three nature trails, including this one through the salt marsh.

The museum is designed to educate and entertain people of all ages and offers in-depth exhibits about the flora and fauna of Cape Cod. Many of the exhibits are interactive, giving children a hands-on experience.

Left: Three major Cape routes, 6, 6A, and 28, converge at Orleans, which make it an active commercial and social center. But just a few steps from the commercial district is this tranquil view of Town Cove.

Above: The architectural gems of Orleans reflect its long and rich history. These Greek revival homes, near the center of town, are typical of the nineteenth century. The home at the bottom is an example of generations adding on to accommodate their growing families.

Above: The Eastham Windmill was built in Plymouth, Massachusetts in 1680 by Thomas Paine, an Eastham resident. It was moved to the Cape in 1770 and to its present location in Eastham in 1808. It now stands proudly as a symbol of the town and is the central feature of the annual Windmill Weekend, held the first weekend after Labor Day.

Right: The bay shore at Eastham and its neighboring towns consists of tidal flats. At high tide they are covered with shallow water, revealing the sand and mud beneath when the waters ebb. These shallows are home to an abundant variety of sea life, including clams, hermit crabs, periwinkles, and small fish, and are favorite feeding grounds for shore birds.

This and previous pages: Marconi Beach offers spectacular views of the Atlantic Ocean along with a little history. The uplands rise some 85 feet above the beach, a fragile cliff that is in constant danger of erosion. It was the site, in 1903, of the first trans-Atlantic radio broadcast. Guglielmo Marconi, an Italian-born inventor, erected an array of four antenna towers at this spot in 1901, a model of which is exhibited under the pavilion. Marconi chose the spot for its unobstructed and elevated access to the ocean...the same thing that attracts visitors today.

A bit north of Eastham is this beautiful spot on the Bay at Wellfleet. With the Cape's miles and miles of beaches, it is still possible to find a place for a solitary walk along the shore, even at the height of the tourist season.

Wellfleet Harbor is home to both pleasure craft and working boats.

Though its population swells in the summer, Wellfleet is a year-round community and home to a rich business and cultural life.

The commercial area offers a number of unique retail outlets and fine dining, and it is only a short hop to an active harbor and wonderful beaches.

At right is the Wellfleet Congregational Church. Founded in 1721, the church's present building on Main Street was constructed in 1850, with the tower rebuilt in 1879 after it was blown over by a storm. The tower holds the town clock, which, appropriately, is equipped with a ship's bells striking system.

Highland Light is situated in North Truro. It was built in 1831, replacing a wooden structure nearby that had been built in 1797 to protect ships in the treacherous seas around Peaked Hill Bars to the Northeast. The staircase and a new lantern were installed in 1840. From the top of the light there is a wonderful view of the ocean and the outermost Cape. Erosion of the beach threatened to overtake the lighthouse, so in 1996 it was moved some 450 feet away from the beach to its present location. A museum and tours of the Highland Light are available to visitors.

Following pages: Coast Guard Beach offers great swimming and surf in the summer months. For the naturalist, it also is accessible to various coastal environments.

Approaching Provincetown you have two choices. On the west, Route 6A goes along the Bay, offering charming views of summer cottages (favorites with area artists) and the vista of the sweeping shoreline, ending in the silhouette of Provincetown. The main road, Route 6, is flanked by the famous sand dunes, rising up between you and the Atlantic Ocean. It is one of the few times in life when you will need to choose between the greatest of two goods!

Not every day on Cape Cod is full of sunshine, and for some of us that is a blessing. When the fog rolls in the world is transformed. To the left is a view of the dunes near Race Point in Provincetown. Above is the Pilgrim Monument, a ghostly reminder that this was the site where the Pilgrims first made landfall in the seventeenth century. It dominates the landscape around Provincetown.

The center of Provincetown is a bustling place, with visitors overrunning the streets of the business area, sharing the roads with cars and the sidewalks with street performers. The harbor at Provincetown is home to the fishing fleet, whale watch boats, and other craft.

To get away from the crowds, walk down Commercial Street to find wonderful art galleries, eateries, and coastal architecture.

A few blocks down Commercial Street, away from the bustle of the harbor and business district, you will be strolling past beautiful old houses and gorgeous gardens, with a gallery of fine art thrown in now and then for good measure. The traffic, both pedestrian and vehicular, is quieter here, and every nook and cranny offers something new and delightful to look at.

The breakwater or dike was built by the Army Corps of Engineers in 1911 to keep sand from flowing into the harbor. The massive boulders provide a delightful way to get from town to the very tip of Cape Cod. The Woods End Lighthouse awaits you at the end of the breakwater, and a little to the left, at the very tip of the Cape, stands its virtual twin, the Long Point Light, which you can also reach by foot.

Above is another view of the Pilgrim Monument. Completed in 1910, the 252-foot tower commemorates the Pilgrims and the time they spent at the tip of the Cape before continuing on to Plymouth. During that time, they wrote and signed the Mayflower Compact. In addition to offering the best view of the Cape, the tower features the informative and interesting Provincetown Museum with exhibits on the Pilgrims, the whaling and fishing industries, and the history of the arts in Provincetown.

Above: Looking up from Oyster Pond in Chatham to the tower of the United Methodist Church.

Right: Stage Harbor Light, Chatham. This 48-foot steel tower was erected in 1880 to guide ships into Stage Harbor. Its light was visible for twelve miles and it served its purpose well until 1933, when it was replaced by an automatic light on a steel frame. Its light removed and tower capped, Stage Harbor Light is now inactive and in private hands.

Lighthouse Beach in Chatham is the largest beach in Chatham. It faces the Atlantic, so the water is cooler and the surf is sometimes wild.

The Chatham Light was built in 1877 and is still an active Coast Guard facility. It has a cast iron shell and a brick lining and stands 48 feet high. Beside it is the keeper's house, also built in 1877.

Left & below: Hyannisport and the surrounding area are a treasure trove of fine Cape architecture. Driving along the coast road you will see these gems and more.

Above & right: Situated above Craigville Beach and Nantucket Sound is a quaint village of private cottages in the gingerbread tradition.

The shore route from Hyannis to Osterville offers many delights, including spectacular settings for Cape homes like this one overlooking a tidal creek, or the cove scene above. Photographed in early spring, the boats anticipate the arrival of summer sailors.

Above: On the Cape it is still possible to find a private beach like this one near Osterville.

Right: Snuggled away above the seagrass, cottages like this one offer spectacular views of the waterfront at Osterville.

Opposite: Saint Barnabas Episcopal Church in Falmouth was founded in 1888. The beautiful edifice of granite and red mountain sandstone was designed in the English country style by Henry Vaughn and completed in June 1890.

Above: Year-round residents join the summer tourists in supporting a thriving and interesting commercial center. A great variety of boutiques and restaurants offers something for everyone.

Right: Throughout Falmouth there are wonderful examples of traditional New England architecture. This grand dame faces the Village Green, where it is one of a number of elegant homes.

Opposite: The view across Shiverick's Pond, looking west toward the First Congregational Church.

Above: Built in 1857 using the timber frame from its previous church building, the First Congregational Church in Falmouth was built in the Greek revival style. The tower was constructed to hold a bell cast for the church by Paul Revere in 1796.

Above: The greatest discoveries on the Cape come when you leave the main roads and take "the road less traveled." In this case the main road is Route 28 between Falmouth and Buzzard's Bay, and the less traveled is the shore road, Route 28A, and its various offshoots. Here you will find quiet spots like this dock near Chappaquoit Point.

Right: The beaches along Buzzard's Bay offer warmer water, calmer seas, and great sweeping vistas, like here at Old Silver Beach.